BURGERS: WHAT'S THE BEEF?

THE DISH ON THE DISH: A HISTORY OF YOUR FAVORITE FOODS

JULIE KNUTSON

Published in the United States of America by Cherry Lake Publishing Group
Ann Arbor, Michigan
www.cherrylakepublishing.com

Reading Adviser: Reading Adviser: Beth Walker Gambro, MS, Ed., Reading Consultant, Yorkville, IL
Photo Credits: © LauriPatterson/iStock.com, cover, 1; © Sergey Nazarov/iStock.com, 5; © VICUSCHKA/Shutterstock.com, 6; © Volha Shakhava/Shutterstock.com, 8; © Oscar C. Williams/Shutterstock.com, 10; © izikMD/Shutterstock.com, 13; © artJazz/iStock.com, 14; © Courtesy of the Library of Congress, LC-DIG-highsm-12949, 17; © Fotosr52/Shutterstock.com, 18; © Kert/Shutterstock.com, 21, 24; © Brent Hofacker/Shutterstock.com, 23; © Nina Firsova/Shutterstock.com, 27; © Alina Sagirova/Shutterstock.com, 28

Copyright © 2022 by Cherry Lake Publishing Group
All rights reserved. No part of this book may be reproduced or utilized in any form or by any means without written permission from the publisher.

Cherry Lake Press is an imprint of Cherry Lake Publishing Group.

Library of Congress Cataloging-in-Publication Data

Names: Knutson, Julie, author.
Title: Burgers: what's the beef? / by Julie Knutson.
Description: Ann Arbor, Michigan : Cherry Lake Publishing, [2022] | Series: The dish on the dish: a history of your favorite foods | Includes index. | Audience: Grades 4-6
Identifiers: LCCN 2021006177 (print) | LCCN 2021006178 (ebook) | ISBN 9781534187290 (hardcover) | ISBN 9781534188693 (paperback) | ISBN 9781534190092 (pdf) | ISBN 9781534191495 (ebook)
Subjects: LCSH: Hamburgers—History—Juvenile literature.
Classification: LCC TX749.5.B43 K68 2021 (print) | LCC TX749.5.B43 (ebook) | DDC 641.6/62—dc23
LC record available at https://lccn.loc.gov/2021006177
LC ebook record available at https://lccn.loc.gov/2021006178

Cherry Lake Publishing Group would like to acknowledge the work of the Partnership for 21st Century Learning, a Network of Battelle for Kids. Please visit http://www.battelleforkids.org/networks/p21 for more information.

Printed in the United States of America
Corporate Graphics

ABOUT THE AUTHOR

Julie Knutson is an author who lives in northern Illinois with her husband, son, and border collie. She prefers her pancakes with Nutella and bananas, her pizza "Detroit-style," and her mac 'n' cheese with little green peas.

TABLE OF CONTENTS

CHAPTER 1
First Plating 4

CHAPTER 2
Migrations 12

CHAPTER 3
Evolution and Wild Variations 20

CHAPTER 4
Make Your Own! 26

FASCINATING FACTS 29
TIMELINE 30
FURTHER READING 31
GLOSSARY 32
INDEX 32

CHAPTER 1

First Plating

Along with the hot dog, this handheld food is the sensation of the summertime barbecue. As a quick drive-through meal, it might put the brakes on hunger during a long family road trip. You can get a very dressed-up version with **Kobe beef** and truffles. Or you can opt for two-bite mini **sliders**. You can also skip the beef entirely and have a plant-based patty made with black beans, chickpeas, or imitation meat.

There are endless varieties, and there are endless ways and settings in which people enjoy them. They are . . . BURGERS!

Sesame buns are a classic vessel for burgers.

In 2007, the James Beard Foundation called the burger America's "most **iconic** food." It's a **staple** item for many. According to an estimate published by *USA Today* in 2019, Americans eat 50 billion burgers each year. That's 156 per person! Oklahoma takes the prize for most consumed **per capita**, at 267. But when and where did people start eating ground beef patties wedged into a bun? And just how did this food become so wildly popular?

[BURGERS: WHAT'S THE BEEF?]

Beef patties are made with simple ingredients like meat, onion, egg, and seasoning.

There are a lot of myths in hamburger history. The most famous is that it was invented in Hamburg, Germany, and arrived on U.S. shores with German immigrants. But there's little evidence to support this claim. A food item made of mixed meats called the Hamburg steak was a common item on German-American restaurant menus in the late 1800s. However, it was served on a plate, not between two slices of bread. It's likely that the name "Hamburg steak" was a way to appeal to consumers. Other German foods from the same time period, including frankfurters and

The Jungle

Can a piece of fiction change the world? In 1906, **muckraker** Upton Sinclair published his novel *The Jungle*, which radically altered how Americans thought about the food they ate.

The book told the tale of an immigrant laborer living in Chicago, Illinois, who endured unclean and unsafe working conditions at a slaughterhouse. *The Jungle*'s vivid descriptions of the meat-packing industry—specifically, of unsafe meat—resulted in a public outcry and demands for change. That same year, the government passed the Federal Meat Inspection Act. The act set regulations for sanitation, monitoring, and inspection of meat plants.

Grilling burger patties over a flame gives them a special flavor.

wieners, were named after central European cities to make the foods sound more exotic and interesting.

    The sandwich started as an upper-class food trend in the 1760s. As legend holds, a Frenchman visiting London spent 24 hours straight playing cards with several English gentlemen. As a way to keep playing without interruption, they were served thinly-sliced beef between two slices of bread. That dish came to be known as the sandwich, after the Earl of Sandwich, one of the men at the table.

Generally served in single-bite portions, the sandwich became a mainstay of upper-class teas and luncheons. According to historian Andrew F. Smith, by the 1770s, English cookbooks included sandwich recipes with fillings like oysters, sausages, prawns, and tongue. By the early 1800s, recipes were appearing in American cookbooks too. While the American upper class continued to eat tiny sandwiches, heartier versions sprung up to meet the appetites of laborers.

In the late 19th century, an important invention paved the way for what we now call the hamburger—the commercial meat grinder. With this development, butchers took scrap meat—sometimes including organs, **gristle**, and excess fat—and quickly ground it into a food product. Some less respectable meat markets sneaked in extenders like flour or oatmeal. Rumors spread that dog, cat, and rat meat were sometimes added, plus chemical preservatives to keep the ground beef looking and smelling fresh. While there was public doubt about the purity of the product, commercially ground meat was cheap and widely available.

Mobile food cart offerings reflected the conditions under which they operated. Food items needed to cook quickly. They also needed to be easy to eat without silverware. Beyond being simple to make and eat, the food had to be cheap. Sausages—what we call hot dogs—were an early favorite. But a new contender soon emerged—ground beef formed into a thin patty and served on a roll. By the 1890s, this "hamburger sandwich" was popping up on menus from coast to coast. And by the early 20th century, it was ready for a new life. It was a hit in school cafeterias, overseas military canteens, and a new type of restaurant that promised speedy but hygienic food.

In 1872, Walter Scott of Providence, Rhode Island, set out to feed night-shift workers at a newspaper printing plant. Scott loaded his pushcart with sandwiches, boiled eggs, and coffee, which he sold outside the factory. The idea caught on in Providence and elsewhere in New England. Soon, innovations like gas grills were added, allowing vendors to serve hot food.

CHAPTER 2

Migrations

In 1916, a Wichita, Kansas, fry cook named Walter Anderson saved up enough money to buy an old shoe repair building. He retooled the space as a hamburger stand and sold 5-cent burgers. Anderson knew that the public didn't fully trust the quality of meat sold at hamburger stands. So, he decided to reassure customers by having fresh beef delivered twice a day. He also prepared the food behind a glass window. This allowed customers to see each and every step of the burger-making process.

As his business grew, Anderson formed a partnership with an insurance broker, Edgar Ingram. In 1921, they launched White Castle®. The design of their chain emphasized cleanliness above all.

Burgers can be topped with many different sauces from ketchup to barbecue.

Tidy, uniformed employees worked against a backdrop of sparkling white tiles. The exterior was modeled after Chicago's Water Tower, one of the few buildings that remained standing after the Great Chicago Fire of 1871. This design was meant to suggest that White Castle® was there to stay. It wasn't long before the chain expanded to other cities, such as St. Louis and Kansas City in Missouri and Omaha, Nebraska. By 1925, White Castle® was serving up 84,000 burgers a year. By 1931, the chain had 131 outlets, most located near factories. And by 1935? White Castle® line cooks were slinging 40 million hamburgers a year!

Classic burger toppings include tomatoes, onions, lettuce, and pickles.

White Castle® launched at a key point in American history. During the 1920s, "machine-age" technologies like radio linked people in all parts of the country. Whether in Texas or Michigan, Oklahoma or Washington, people all listened to the same **syndicated** mystery, comedy, and music shows. They heard similar products advertised and saw cars overtake their roadways. It was a consumer-driven moment. Recognizing that there were no "American foods" as yet, clever **entrepreneurs** set out to build a culinary culture. The hamburger became a key player in this drama.

Production Line Foods

Henry Ford revolutionized the American factory with the **assembly line**. This method of building cars meant that each worker fulfilled a specific, repetitive role. The technique led to a huge increase in efficiency. A car that once took 12 hours to build could be built in 1.5 hours using assembly-line labor!

Fast-food pioneers borrowed from Ford, using kitchen production line methods to make service efficient and keep costs low. White Castle®'s founders were early adopters of these tactics. In the late 1940s, the McDonald brothers built their restaurant around Ford's ideas. With specific employees doing only one assigned task—filling drinks, flipping burgers, bagging sandwiches—record numbers of customers could be served.

In the 1950s, carhop dining was extremely popular. This type of dining involves servers bringing food to people in their cars.

From factory-made cheese to processed meats, the **Industrial Revolution** gave the world new ways of making food. The same revolution also created new needs regarding food. Factory laborers often worked far from home. Their work shifts could be any time during the day or night. For many workers, it wasn't possible to go home for lunch or dinner. While some factories had cafeterias to serve daytime shifts, these lunchrooms often closed at night. How to solve this problem? Enter enterprising street vendors who operated lunch wagons.

The "little burger that could" kept trucking along, even during the tough times of the 1930s and 1940s. At the peak of the **Great Depression**, it offered an affordable meal to many. It was an item people could rely on. In nearly any town across the country, consumers could expect to find it on menus. As the United States entered World War II in 1941, burgers offered a cheap and easy way to feed hungry overseas troops. On the home front, beef was **rationed**. Fast food restaurant owners developed cheaper menu items like french fries and fried egg sandwiches to feed customers while meat was in short supply. Those menu items remained popular well after the war's end.

After World War II, the hamburger entered a golden age . . . one helped along by the "Golden Arches" of McDonald's®. Brothers Richard and Maurice McDonald moved from New Hampshire to sunny Los Angeles, California, in the early 1930s. They dreamed of making it big in entertainment. They opened a movie theater.

McDonald's® first **franchise** location opened in Des Plaines, Illinois, in 1955.

That plan didn't work, so they shifted their focus to food. In 1940, they uprooted from Los Angeles, California, and headed about 100 miles (161 kilometers) east to San Bernardino, California. There, they opened a burger and barbecue restaurant. Business was good . . . but they thought it could be better.

In 1948, the brothers revamped their business for maximum efficiency. Business boomed. Their success wasn't unnoticed. Magazines featured their 15-cent burgers that came with two pickle slices, ketchup, and chopped onion. Other entrepreneurs

The term "sliders" for miniature burgers originated in the 1940s.

wanting to launch their own franchises came too. These included the founders of Carl's Jr.®, Kentucky Fried Chicken®, and Burger King®. A curious milkshake machine salesman from Illinois also traveled to San Bernardino, California. His name was Ray Kroc, and he eventually bought the rights to expand the McDonald's® empire outside of Southern California.

The idea that McDonald's® could promise people the exact *same* food and experience at every location helped the chain grow.

By the end of 1959, there were 100 outlets. In 1961, the company established a "Hamburger University" to train franchise owners on brand standards and operations. By 1963, McDonald's® was putting 1 million burgers into the hands, mouths, and stomachs of consumers every day. It spawned several other chains that hoped to achieve the same success. Each of these new chains tried to find their own place in the booming burger market. Where do things stand today for McDonald's®? According to the corporate website, the company operates about 34,000 restaurants in 118 countries, serving more than 69 million people every day.

But lots of chefs and culinary scientists are pushing to take the burger beyond basic **condiments** and drive-through windows. What's next for the burger? Keep reading to find out!

*In the 1960s, civil rights activists fought to **desegregate** public spaces. These included fast-food restaurants like McDonald's®, which, according to historian Marcia Chatelain, often refused to serve Black customers or served them at "Colored-Only" pick-up windows. Some White franchise owners even closed restaurants in Black communities. This led McDonald's® to recruit Black business owners for franchises, including Herman Petty of Chicago, Illinois. Petty opened the first Black-owned McDonald's® in the United States on December 21, 1968.*

CHAPTER 3

Evolution and Wild Variations

For better and for worse, the food we eat reflects the world in which we live. Restaurant menus mirror the wants, needs, and concerns of customers. Whether at a local food truck or at a fast-food chain, we can learn a lot about people's cultures and beliefs by what they put on their plates. Demand for new plant-based burger products like the Impossible™ Burger shows that many people still want to enjoy this classic sandwich . . . just without the meat. Others want to push the burger's boundaries, constructing larger and even more outrageous versions.

This avocado burger features quinoa, sweet potato, sun dried tomatoes, and beet pesto.

So, let's take a trip around the world to see what's expected of a burger in different places!

While the hamburger may be the most iconic food in the United States, that doesn't mean you'll get the same burger in Miami, Florida, as in Minneapolis, Minnesota. Regional identities show up in the kitchen. In Florida, the *frita Cubana* is topped with crispy potato sticks, diced onion, and ketchup. As you'd likely guess, this sandwich is a Cuban import reflecting the roots of many people in southern Florida. In the dairy-rich Midwest, cheese is sometimes stuffed into the middle of the burger rather than placed on top of it.

From start to finish, beef production places a major strain on the environment. As reported by the British Broadcasting Corporation (BBC), cattle account for about 14 percent of all greenhouse emissions from human activities. Beyond that, livestock farming requires huge amounts of water. It takes 4,227 gallons (16,000 liters) of water to produce 2.2 pounds (1 kilogram) of grain-fed beef. That compares to 37 gallons (140 L) for a cup of coffee and 264 gallons (1,000 L) for 34 ounces (946 grams) of milk.

Poutine burgers are topped with cheese curds, french fries, and gravy.

The effect? It's a bit like biting into a cupcake filled with a hidden surprise of frosting . . . except the surprise in this case is melted cheese.

In Canada, the Hot Hamburg sandwich is like a burger and **poutine** mash-up. This messy creation slathers the burger in gravy. Green peas and french fries round out the plate, which definitely requires a fork and knife.

Journey across the Pacific Ocean to Japan! The chain MOS Burger™ launched in 1972, just 1 year after McDonald's® opened its first restaurant in the country. MOS didn't try to copy McDonald's®. Instead of speed, quality and safety were put at the forefront.

[BURGERS: WHAT'S THE BEEF?]

This vegan chickpea burger features a guacamole sauce.

Today, you can eat at MOS Burgers™ throughout East Asia, enjoying a signature Teriyaki Burger sandwiched between two rice cakes. As a side, you can add mussel nuggets or fried prawns.

Further southwest in the Pacific, New Zealand offers its own signature burger. The "Kiwi Burger" was inspired by a salad of lettuce, beets, egg, and ham. In the burger version, all of these ingredients are loaded—you guessed it—atop a beef patty and wedged between a bun. And don't forget the tomato, cheese, onions, mustard, and ketchup!

Next, let's travel north to India, where nearly 80 percent of the population is Hindu. In this religious tradition, cows are considered a sacred symbol of life. They aren't eaten. But fear not, beef substitutes abound! Fast-food chain Nirula's serves lamb, chicken, and vegetable-based patties dressed with toppings like mint-tamarind sauce.

Our last stop is Brazil, the world's largest beef-producing country. Believe it or not, Brazil's oldest fast-food chain was founded in 1952 by American championship tennis player Bob Falkenburg. Today, Bob's is still serving burgers like the "Big Bob," which is made of two beef patties, onions, and leaf chicory. Had your share of beef at this point? Opt for a grilled cheese sandwich with sliced bananas instead.

The world's first lab-grown burger was cooked and eaten in August 2013. Scientists at Maastricht University in the Netherlands cultured the meat from the cells of a cow. Why do this? Lab-grown beef uses much less energy and land and produces less carbon than farmed livestock.

CHAPTER 4

Make Your Own!

What does your ideal burger involve? Is it made of beef or mashed black beans? Topped with guacamole or stuffed with pimento cheese? Served on a sesame bun or wrapped in lettuce leaves?

Along with an adult helper, test out this veggie version. And add spices and toppings to your taste!

INGREDIENTS:

- 1 15.5 ounce (439 gram) can chickpeas
- 1½ cups (192 g) carrots
- ⅓ cup (43 g) peas
- ¼ cup (32 g) corn
- 1½ cups (192 g) cabbage
- 1 cup (128 g) cauliflower or broccoli
- ¼ teaspoon (1.4 g) turmeric
- ½ teaspoon (2.8 g) chili powder
- 1 tablespoon (17 g) Italian mixed herb
- 1½ teaspoons (7 milliliters) olive oil
- ¼ cup (60 ml) water
- 2 tablespoons (34 g) flour

Just like beef burgers, veggie burgers can be topped with just about anything!

DIRECTIONS:

1. Put all the vegetables—including the chickpeas—into a food processor or blender. Pulse, but leave some texture!

2. Have an adult heat a skillet over medium heat. Add oil, and pour the veggie mix into the pan. Sprinkle with any desired spices, stir regularly, and cook for 8 to 10 minutes.

3. Allow the mixture to cool.

4. After the mixture has reached room temperature, scoop out spoonfuls and form into patties. Place the patties on a parchment-lined baking sheet.

5. Refrigerate the patties for 30 minutes.

6. Mix flour and water in a small bowl.

7. Have an adult heat oil in another frying pan over medium-low heat.

8. Dip each patty in the flour and water mix. Have an adult add the patties to the heated pan. Cook for about 4 minutes on each side.

9. Serve in a bun with condiments of your choice!

[BURGERS: WHAT'S THE BEEF?]

Many restaurants offer burgers on their menus.

Flipping 10 Fascinating Facts on Burgers

- Just how many burgers do Americans eat per year? If all those hamburgers were arranged in a line, it would circle the planet more than 32 times.

- May 28 is National Hamburger Day in the United States.

- McDonald's® Golden Arches are one of the most recognizable symbols in the world.

- McDonald's® serves 75 burgers every second and is the world's largest distributor of toys.

- In 1996, McDonald's® estimated that one in eight Americans had worked in one of its restaurants. Former employees include Amazon founder Jeff Bezos, singer Shania Twain, and actor-director Lin-Manuel Miranda.

- At Mallie's Sports Grill & Bar in Michigan, you can order the "Absolutely Ridiculous Burger," the world's largest commercially sold hamburger. This monster burger weighs in at 150 pounds (68 kg) and costs $399.

- The world's largest burger restaurant, I'M Hungry, is located in Jeddah, Saudi Arabia. It's about the size of 11 tennis courts.

- According to *Guinness World Records*, the fastest burger made of Play-Doh® was created in 23.53 seconds by 9-year-old Luo Jingjing.

- In October 2019, 1,047 people gathered in Spain to make the largest ever "human image of a burger" at Madrid's Goiko Grill. They formed a burger shape using their bodies.

- Because "Hamburg" was associated with Germany, hamburgers were renamed "Liberty Sandwiches" during World War I.

Timeline

1872 Rhode Island food seller Walter Scott sets out to feed the night shift at a newspaper plant.

1876 The commercial meat grinder is a sensation at the Philadelphia Centennial Exposition in Pennsylvania. A German-themed restaurant at this fair features a hit menu item made with ground beef, the Hamburg steak.

1906 Upton Sinclair's *The Jungle* leads to the reform of the meat-packing industry.

1921 The first White Castle® restaurant opens.

1948 The McDonald brothers revamp their San Bernardino, California, restaurant for maximum efficiency.

1961 McDonald's® launches Hamburger University to train franchisees. Two years later, Burger King® opens Whopper College for the same purpose.

1966 Ronald McDonald becomes the McDonald's® spokesperson.

1993 The soy-based BOCA Burger debuts as a vegetarian alternative to the beef patty.

2002 Two teens sue McDonald's® on the claim that the chain's food made them obese.

2020 Cultured meat begins to move from the laboratory to the table, as lab-grown chicken is served at a restaurant in Singapore.

GLOSSARY

assembly line (uh-SEM-blee LINE) a way of assembling goods to increase efficiency

condiments (KON-duh-muhnts) things that enhance food flavor, such as ketchup or mustard

desegregate (dee-SEG-ruh-gate) to end policies of racial segregation

entrepreneurs (on-truh-pruh-NURZ) people who start businesses or create products

franchise (FRAN-chize) a company's license to an individual to own and operate one of their businesses

Great Depression (GRAYT di-PRESH-uhn) the period of global economic decline that lasted from 1929 until 1939

gristle (GRISS-uhl) tough cartilage tissue in meat

iconic (eye-KON-ik) famous and widely recognized

Industrial Revolution (in-DUHSS-tree-uhl rev-uh-LOO-shuhn) the large social and economic shift toward machine and factory-produced goods

Kobe beef (KOH-bee BEEF) prized specialty beef from Japanese cattle

muckraker (MUK-ray-kuhr) a reporter who exposed corruption

per capita (PUHR KAH-puh-tuh) the number for each person

poutine (poo-TEEN) french fries topped with cheese curds and gravy, commonly served in Canada

rationed (RASH-uhnd) when each person can have only a fixed amount of something, especially when resources need to be conserved

sliders (SLY-duhrs) mini burgers

staple (STAY-puhl) a core element of a diet

syndicated (SIN-duh-kay-tuhd) broadcast through a number of media outlets

INDEX

Anderson, Walter, 12–13
assembly-line production, 15
avocado burger, 21

beef production, 22, 25
Blacks, 19
Bob's, 25
BOCA Burger, 30
Brazil, 25
Burger King®, 18, 30
burgers
    consumption, 5, 19, 29
    early 20th century, 11
    facts about, 29
    grilling, 8
    history of, 7–11
    lab-grown, 25, 30
    overview, 4–11
    plant-based, 4, 20, 25, 26–27, 30
    records, 29
    spread of popularity, 12–19
    variations around the world, 20–25
    vegan, 24
    during WW II, 16

Canada, 23
carhop dining, 10
Carl's Jr.®, 18
cheese, 22–23

factories, 10, 11, 30
fast-food restaurants, 15, 19
Florida, 22
Ford, Henry, 15
franchises, 18
frita Cubana, 22

Germany, 7–8, 29
greenhouse emissions, 22

Impossible™ Burger, 20
India, 25
Industrial Revolution, 10
Ingram, Edgar, 12–13

Japan, 23–24
Jungle, The (Sinclair), 7, 30

Kentucky Fried Chicken®, 18
Kiwi Burger, 24
Kroc, Ray, 18

lunch wagons, 10–11

McDonald's®, 15, 16–19, 29, 30
meat grinder, 9, 30
meat-packing industry, 7, 30
MOS Burger™, 23–24

New Zealand, 24
Nirula's, 25

poutine burgers, 23

recipe, 26–27

sandwiches, 8–9
Saudi Arabia, 29
Sinclair, Upton, 7, 30
sliders, 4, 18

timeline, 30
toppings, 13, 14

White Castle®, 12–13, 15, 30
Wichita, KS, 12

32   [21ST CENTURY SKILLS LIBRARY]

Further Reading

BOOKS

Kuskowski, Alex. *Cool Hamburger Recipes: Main Dishes for Beginning Chefs.* Minneapolis, MN: ABDO Publishing, 2017.

Senker, Cath. *McDonald's: The Business behind the Golden Arches.* Minneapolis, MN: Lerner Publishing, 2016.

Sullivan, Jaclyn. *What's in Your Hamburger?* New York, NY: PowerKids Press, 2012.

WEBSITE

Wonderopolis—Why Aren't Hamburgers Made Of Ham?
www.wonderopolis.org/wonder/why-aren-t-hamburgers-made-of-ham
Check out this website to learn about hamburgers.